Things I Heard Myself Say

Insights From a Candid Interview with Yourself

Eli Boulous

with Curtis L. Odom, Ed.D.

THINGS I HEARD MYSELF SAY

INSIGHTS FROM A CANDID INTERVIEW WITH YOURSELF

ELI BOULOUS

WITH CURTIS L. ODOM, ED.D.

ISBN 9798986085906

PUBLISHED BY BOOKNOLOGY
(A Business & Educational Imprint from Adducent)
www.AdducentCreative.com
Jacksonville, Florida USA
Published in the United States of America

Editing Note from the publisher: *THINGS I HEARD MYSELF SAY: INSIGHTS FROM A CANDID INTERVIEW WITH YOURSELF* is written conversationally and left so intentionally. That means it has not been reworked to change casual word choice, usage, phrasing, or to remove the personal tone of a talk between the authors and readers.

Listen Closely to Your Own Answers!

THINGS I HEARD MYSELF SAY

INSIGHTS FROM A CANDID INTERVIEW WITH YOURSELF

Justin,

Wishing you only happiness & success on your career journey! I hope this journal helps you better the person most important to your career's success - you!

To Our Success,

Eli Brael

ACKNOWLEDGMENTS

My first acknowledgment goes to Riley A., and Nick S. Because of your glowing recommendations to take Dr. Curtis Odom's Organizational Behavior course, all of this is possible. I could have never expected what was to come from that class. I'm forever grateful to you two for this, as well as all of the experiences and memories we've shared together. Here's to many more years of friendship, laughs, and success!

To all of the readers of *Things I Heard My Professor Say* - thank you for turning the impact of a single college course into purposeful and uplifting material to help everyone live a more authentic and successful life. We could never have imagined the reception we received after releasing that book - you have no idea of the joy and fulfillment your responses gave to me and Dr. Odom - thank you!

Finally, I want to send a special thanks to Courtney R., Ike J., Elijah K., Vanessa B., Jody P., Austin S., Michael AJ., Filippo G., Aiman H., Derek VDN., and Simon B. for your help in making this book possible! Your input and insights shared directly culminated in the construction of this book. We appreciate you and your willingness to empower the next generation of leaders!

As Dr. Odom famously signs all of his correspondence...

To Our Success!

DEDICATION

To my parents, Paul and Vanessa. Your examples of hard work, compassion, exploration, and understanding made it easy from a young age to be the best version of myself.

Thank you for giving me the trust, confidence, and freedom to go out and discover the world on my own. In doing so, I have been fortunate enough to create a life full of meaningful connections, empowering work, and unforgettable experiences.

Without your love and support, none of this would be possible.

My love now and forever,

Elias

TABLE OF CONTENTS

PREFACE

The idea for this book came from spending time talking with many who enjoyed reading over 30 years of lessons learned found in our preceding book, *Things I Heard My Professor Say*. From those insightful conversations, we learned that many people need a career journal where they, as the reader, go through the process of navigating and assessing the major stages of their career – written in their own words by their own hand.

The need people have for a career journal is reinforced by my experiences as a professor. The best professional title I'll ever have is professor because, with that title, I get to be surrounded by really smart, savvy students. But I also get to meet and know students who don't have someone they can talk to about how to make career choices. Each week I have at least one student make an office hours appointment, but they do not want to talk about the upcoming paper or group assignment that is due. Instead, they come seeking career advice. But I do not tell them which career to choose. I talk with them about how to choose their own career for themselves.

Students know that they can talk to me about their career, ask me about my career, talk to me about their job search, or even strategize about a pending job interview. Students will open up to me and say, "Professor, I don't know what I should be doing. I don't know where my career is going to go. I am only majoring in this subject because my parents told me to or because they think it will make me the most money right out of college. But I don't know what I really want to do. How did you get started? Did you know what you wanted to do at age 21? What advice can you give me? What do you think I should do?"

These are the conversations that I have every week of each semester. Students visit with me in my office, and I give them what I jokingly call 'the true Hollywood story' of personal success – that there is no single definition of success. The guidance that I give to each of these students is that if they don't know what they want to do, then they should at least know what they DON'T want to do. Most of these students have never thought about owning their career choices in that way. They have never had this internal conversation with themselves where they can hear their truth spoken.

As we thought more about how to create what the readers of *Things I Heard My Professor Say* wanted next, Eli and I started talking to our contemporaries and asking them, "Did you enjoy our first book? What book do you need right now? What book should we have written? What book should we write next?" What came out of those conversations is that most of the people we spoke to talked about needing career coaching or wanting personalized career advice. They spoke to us of their need for a thinking tool, a notebook, a journal, or a pocket guide where they could find and capture pragmatic career insights. They spoke of needing personalized help with preparing for their next job interview with questions and prompts tailored to this moment in time and to this current intersection of their work and life.

Each chapter became five quotes with four prompts attributed to that quote. The result was that for each stage of your career, we give you 20 questions to ask yourself and those answers become your career compass to help you find the next stage of your career or your career journal to use while you reflect on your previous career stage now fading in the rearview mirror.

We sat on this plan for a moment, and the potential impact of the opportunity became clear. Our next book should be the opportunity for us to take *Things I Heard My Professor Say* to the next level.

What if we enabled the reader to create a journal of answers to job interview questions where the reader interviews themself? The answers then written by the reader in the whitespace on the pages of the book would become their personalized preparation for identifying, delivering, evaluating, broadening, and fostering their last, current, and next career opportunities. What if the book we were thinking about writing was THAT journal for the reader to capture the things they heard themself say? And in our asking that question out loud, the book title was born: *Things I Heard Myself Say - Insights From A Candid Interview With Yourself.* At that moment, we realized that this book was what people needed – a personalized career journal for the reader created by the reader.

This book, *Things I Heard Myself Say,* was initially planned to give 20-somethings and 30-somethings a tool that they could put to immediate use. But as we thought about this deeper, we realized that people at any stage of their career would benefit from using this book to quiet the noise that has been drowning out their internal career conversation. Many of us have let external conversations about career create who we are now in work and life. Some just didn't have the right interview questions to ask themselves to better understand answers based on their own personality, preference, or perspective. We believe that this inner dialogue approach to finding your career success will have a wide appeal to an audience who is interested in thinking about what they are thinking about.

With that direction, we went all-in, trying to create the perfect book to start or continue the inner dialogue with yourself as the reader to get you to think about what you need to change or want to do differently as the owner of your career. The further we travel on our career journey, the more frequently we turn to our inner dialogue for navigation. Having a candid interview with ourselves could be the key to finding or creating our chosen career path. Yet even this very personal discussion may benefit from a gentle push or a deliberate nudge forward while we go about capturing our own thoughts and realizations in the form of a personalized career journal.

Things I Heard Myself Say as a concept is a book meant to deliberately plug into the zeitgeist of the modern workforce. This personalized career journal is our effort to give you as a prior reader of *Things I Heard My Professor Say* what you have not had before. A book that gives you a place to ask yourself interview questions and the space to capture your answers in a private personal journal to use over and over again as you navigate your career. And by having time in advance to think through your answers to these questions and prompts, we can help you prevent that awkward moment in your next job interview when you would have given a less than authentic answer and then had to listen to yourself not speak your truth.

In your hands is the book you told us that you wanted and needed. *Things I Heard Myself Say* is a curated collection of quotes, questions, prompts, and your answers. It is your personalized career journal created in part by you as the reader that is full of tested conversation starters for a candid interview with the person you need to know best – yourself. Listen closely to your own answers.

To Our Success!

How You Can Get the Most Out of This Book

1. Find a quiet place where you can think freely and honestly.
2. Put yourself in a headspace where you're ready to be interviewed rather than just sit and read!
3. Open to the section that has the questions you feel most ready to answer at this time.
4. Answer prompts openly and honestly; don't be discouraged if you have a tough time responding or you don't like your answers. This is all to help with self-understanding - your self-understanding!
5. Write down your answers to help you prepare for the strides you're looking to make in your career!
6. Set a reminder to revisit the book often to see how your actions align with the answers you've put to paper.
7. Remember that this book is now a career journal for YOU and only YOU.

IDENTIFYING YOUR NEXT OPPORTUNITY

So, if you really believe in emotional intelligence, it starts with self-awareness. Only with self-awareness or feedback given to you can you then self-manage. Self-Management leads to being socially aware, which is imperative when it comes to how others see you. Then you ask: how do I go about getting the job? First job, second job, last job, side job...whatever! What's the preparation that has to go into that? There are plenty of times when people will try to get a job because it's what they think they should have as the job. But it's not actually the work that they want to do. Or they go and get a job in a place where everyone tells them that that's where they need to be, but then they realize it's not for them.

As you think about what could be the next opportunity for yourself, what does that look like, and how will you go about getting it? Use the quotes and prompts on the following pages to help you turn these thoughts into vision and action.

THE FOUR THINGS PEOPLE WANT FROM A JOB:

1. **To be welcomed.**
2. **To feel valued.**
3. **To be able to contribute.**
4. **To be their authentic self.**

The best organizations are those organizations that will be seen as the best places to work. They'll meet that person as their authentic self and, in doing so, allow them to feel welcomed, valued, and able to contribute. *If you can get three of the four or four of the four, it's an ideal place to be.* Most places where people only find one, that's a cue to leave that place.

a. When were you most satisfied in a previous job?

b. Where do you want to go to work every day?

c. What three things are most important to you in your job?

d. What would be your ideal working environment?

INTENSITY, PERSISTENCE, AND DIRECTION ARE...

Wasted without being part of a plan attached to a goal.

People can be busy and not be productive. The one that I would say really is the most important is direction. I mean, you can be intense and persistent, but those things wane based on people's energy and mood. *So, the fact that you'd go after something without really having a goal, where you go after certain tactics, they are not linked together. That's really not helpful.* And you know, it ultimately turns into admirable but wasted energy.

a. Talk about a time when you showed real determination.

b. Do you find it difficult to adapt to new situations?

c. What techniques and tools do you use to keep yourself organized?

d. How do you plan to achieve your career goals?

IF YOU ARE NOT WILLING TO LOSE EVERYTHING FOR SOMETHING...

Then you cannot truly win at anything.

You know what, I can go on from this job that I was in to another job where again, I wouldn't fit in, or wouldn't fit the mold, or where I would again have to deny who I was, where I have to again risk not being welcomed and valued and able to contribute being my authentic self," or I can say, "You know what, I'm going to go all-in on myself." And I said, "You know what? I'm just going to double down on me and go all-in." And that risk of going out on my own has paid off now, ten plus years later. *I believe that I have won because I get to go to work every day doing exactly what I want to do, where I want to do it, when I want to do it, with whom, and how.* And if I didn't take the opportunity to go all-in on myself, then you know, I wouldn't be here.

a. What career accomplishment makes you most proud?

b. What would you attempt to do if you knew you couldn't fail?

c. What has been the most rewarding experience of your career thus far?

d. What do you ultimately want to become?

IF YOU DON'T LEARN HOW TO FAIL...

You won't know how to appreciate success when it arrives.

If you don't believe the acronym FAIL means 'First Attempt In Learning,' then you can't really grow. *You can't find success until you've experienced failure.* Because it's almost like tasting fruit that you've only seen but never actually tasted. When you have failed and failed, and you get that taste of success, it is so reaffirming. It is so comforting, and it makes you willing to fail again.

a. Tell me about a time you had to manage a particularly heavy workload. How did you handle it?

b. How have you responded to career/life failures previously?

c. Can you work under pressure?

d. Do you consider yourself successful?

NETWORKING ELEVATOR PITCH:

Who you are, what you do, how you are different from anyone else who does that, and how you would help the company smart enough to hire you.

"That last one will differentiate you because most people are only out here looking for the job and only looking for what the employer can do for them. *No one's out here saying, 'Listen, if you hired me, this is what I'm going to do for you'"*.

a. Who are you?

b. What do you do in regards to work/experiences?

c. How are you different from anyone else who does that?

d. How would you help the company smart enough to hire you?

You're in this job hunt, you really want these things, and now you've explained it to yourself in the last few pages. Beyond answering the prompts, what are you proud of? What about yourself do you love? Stop and take a moment to appreciate yourself for taking this inward journey!

Think about how you're going to succeed and what success will look like in the job in the next section.

Delivering In Your Current Opportunity

"I'm going after the job, I get it, and I've started. Now, I get there, and I've got to be successful in that role." Think of a three-part plan. Part 1 is all about discovery. Discovering a job, discovering a role, discovering the people, discovering what is really asked of me. Part 2 is all about delivery. You got to deliver. You got to deliver, you got to get results, you got to get the job done. Part 3 is all about deciding. Part 3 is like, "Okay, do I want to stay here or do I not? Am I being groomed in the way that I want to, or am I not? Have I gotten success enough where it looks like I am on a path to being promoted or not?"

This section is all about setting yourself up to excel in this role that you really wanted. As you go through this section, reflect on what you want to get out of this opportunity. What skills, knowledge, and ability do you want to come out of this with? Keep these thoughts close as you venture into the next section.

IN YOUR FIRST 90 DAYS...

In a new position or with a new organization, your primary job is to look, listen, and learn.

When you move into a new job, whether it's a new company or a new role within your company, you can't just assume that you could just jump right into it and get results and have an impact. You don't know the players. You don't know the culture. But in the business environment, the corporate environment, I realized that, you know what? *Let me assess where I just landed to figure out what is the terrain, which direction do I need to go, and what are the mile markers or the things that I need to see that are going to guide me?*

a. Think of a time you learned from one of your peers as you began a job. What did you do to make the learning easier for yourself?

b. What's your work style?

c. Are you a personal goal-setter at work, or do you generally follow a routine, and why?

d. What makes you unique?

ONLY FEEDBACK CAN CLOSE OUR BLIND SPOTS.

Only by receiving both constructive and confirming feedback can our personal and professional growth occur.

People will only give you feedback if they care about your success. If people are not committed to your success, they're not going to give you feedback. The personal growth came when I realized the people who gave me the most difficult feedback gave it to me because they cared about me as a person, and they wanted to see me successful.

a. What assignment was too difficult for you, and how did you resolve the issue?

b. Give me an example of a time you did something wrong. How did you handle it?

c. What was the last project you led, and what was the outcome?

d. Can you tell us about a project or accomplishment you're proud of and why?

SOMETIMES THE BEST THING TO DO…

In a situation is nothing at all. Especially when your initial reaction to an ask or a presented opportunity does not elicit a "Hell yes!" as your response.

What I have learned is the power of the pause. There's power in not responding to an email right away. There's power in waiting to respond until you've had a good night's sleep or you've had a chance to rest. You know, sometimes doing nothing is the best thing. *To say no and why, or to say, you know, instead of no, 'Not right now.' That is also a very powerful thing to say.* "I'm not saying no, but I'm saying not right now." "I'm not ready right now. I don't have the resources. I don't have the knowledge or skill." I think 'no' with an explanation is powerful.

a. How do you prioritize your work?

b. What are your pet peeves?

c. What motivates you?

d. What causes are you passionate about?

STRESS COMES FROM…

Spending too much time trying to be someone you're not, or doing something you really don't want to be doing.

It was all about being in a job that I had taken because it was part of achieving a goal. I didn't look at the red flags. I didn't look at the stop signs. I was head down, charging toward a goal, even though I was running through a field of landmines. *And what I found is, when I got to that place, that I had to become someone I wasn't in order to stay employed.* And that works for a while. And I mean, anybody can be on their best behavior for about six months. I'm no longer going to try to fit into a mold that was never crafted for me." The stress fell away. There were other stresses, or certainly the stress of starting a business, you know, that's not something to be taken lightly. But even in the toughest moments of being an entrepreneur, and the toughest moments of wondering if the business was going to succeed or fold, I didn't have the stress of trying to figure out who I needed to be in the moment. I just was myself and as we talked about, betting on myself was the best thing I could have done.

a. Describe a time when you had to work with someone whose personality or work style was very different from yours.

b. How do you deal with pressure or stressful situations?

c. Talk about a work environment that you think would be ineffective for you.

d. What makes you uncomfortable?

NO MATTER WHAT YOU DO FOR WORK...

You were hired to get results. Never forget that you only get to keep your job by getting measurable results.

I've seen plenty of people go into the office and try to work on being well-liked without being productive, without getting results. You know, bonuses are tied to results. Promotions are tied to results. *To lose sight of that, or not be told that, puts people at a disadvantage because if you don't know what is expected of you, then you can't go after achieving those expectations.*

a. Tell me about a time when you had to adapt to change.

b. Do you like to ask questions or try to figure things out on your own, and why?

c. Do you consider yourself a big-picture person or a detail-oriented person?

d. If someone asked you, "What results have you gotten in your career?" What would you say?

Since you've done so well in the job you strived for, you're probably going to want to be promoted to continue your career trajectory. Even though you've done very well in the job, that doesn't lock you in for a promotion. Prepare for taking that next step in your journey in the next section.

ELEVATING YOUR PROFESSIONAL IMPACT

"You know what? Do I really want to be promoted, or do I just want to make more money?" It's not the same thing. Most people get to the height of being an individual contributor, and then the only next thing for them is to be promoted. And they become someone who is now being asked to lead people, and now they're in a leadership role without any leadership skills. And then that's a challenge because you're on full display. Leaders are always on stage. And if you don't have the skills, I'm going to be able to see that from a mile away. You can't hide from it.

So, where do you want to go from here? Do you want to manage and lead people? Or do you want to become a subject matter expert in the work you're already doing without the responsibility of managing a team of people? Maybe you want to join a new team and expand your skill sets. There is no right or wrong answer, but keep these paths in mind as you go through this third section.

IF YOU CAN'T BE REPLACED, YOU CAN'T BE PROMOTED.

If I'm a leader of a team or I'm a manager, and I have somebody on my team that performs a critical job, but no one else can do that, even if there's a next promotion open and I know you're ready for it and that you should have it, I'm not going to promote you because to promote you leaves a hole in the organization. *I can't afford to promote you into this new role and leave a gaping hole in this other role. I'd much rather find somebody for this role* because you have made yourself, unfortunately, indispensable and irreplaceable.

a. Is there something you can do in your role that no one else can do? If so, would it prevent you from being promoted from the role? If not, what skill/ability makes you stand out in that role?

b. Talk about being on a team when someone didn't pull their weight? How did you handle it?

c. How would you feel about working for someone who knows less than you?

d. How can you help the organization make sure you're not the only one who can do your job?

STAYING AT ONE COMPANY SHOULD MEAN…

That you have continually received new opportunities for growth, not from being afraid to find new opportunities elsewhere.

I've met people along the way who have been with a company for 30 years or 40 years. I've always been curious as to how they stayed for that long. And the answer that I always got from people who were in that space was, *"I've had many jobs, but with one employer. I've always felt like I've been moving and growing and getting more responsibility."* That's the answer that works. What I think about that is that to have one employer but be able to have multiple ways of contributing that's what many people want.

a. Tell me something you've learned recently.

b. What's one challenge you've faced, and how did you overcome it?

c. Talk about a situation where you took initiative or took on a leadership role.

d. What would you consider a deal-breaker for you with your current company?

THE MARK OF AN EMPOWERING LEADER IS...

One who tells you what needs to be done, when it needs to be done, where it needs to be done, and why it needs to be done. They will never tell you how it needs to be done.

"Listen, I hired you for your knowledge, skill, and ability. And my job is to help you be successful. To tell you what I need, when I need it, where it needs to happen, when, and sometimes with who. *But I don't want to hire you if I have to tell you how to do the job. Because if I have to tell you how, then I might as well do your job for you, which means I don't need you.*" And by allowing me to have the how, it allowed me to be creative. It allowed me to be innovative. There's more: do it whichever way you think it's going to work, but then explain to me how you did it and the rationale behind it.

a. How would your current boss describe you?

b. Describe a time when your boss was wrong. How did you handle the situation?

c. Are you more of a leader or a follower?

d. Who has impacted you most in your career, and how?

WITHOUT FAILURE AND LEARNING FROM THAT FAILURE...

There can be no innovation.

I'm talking about risking discomfort. You don't get it right the first time. Failing means maybe you need three or four times to get it right. *How can you go where you've never been before, do what you've never done before, without being willing to take a risk?* It doesn't work.

a. Talk about a time you had to learn something completely new.

b. Tell me about a time when you weren't sure how to do something. How did you go about seeking out information?

c. What critical feedback do you most often receive?

d. What was your greatest failure, and what did you learn from it?

CONSISTENTLY UPDATE YOUR MINDSET, SKILLSET, AND TOOLSET.

That's the way to increase your value to an organization and increase your career opportunities.

People are compensated for their time and their talent. *The only way to increase your compensation is either increase the amount of time you spend doing the work or increase your talent, which means that your talent is worth more.* In that environment, only increasing your talent, your mindset, skillset, toolset, looking to see what does the organization need more of that it doesn't have, looking to see what are the skills that are in vogue, what are the things that people are looking for to be brought into the organization, and figure out how do you either upskill or re-skill yourself to be able to have that.

a. Describe a time when your work was criticized.

b. What are three skills or traits you wish you had?

c. How do you want to improve yourself in the next year?

d. Do you have a mentor?

It's okay to not be fully 100% positive on all these answers. This is your chance to understand yourself, first and foremost. That's the point of this interview. It's not to be negative toward yourself. Learn from this. We just asked a lot of you. You're asking a lot of yourself just to do this, just to answer these questions. We know your brain is smoking right now. Take a breather and smile because you are setting yourself up for a more fulfilling life by interviewing yourself!

BROADENING YOUR CAREER SCOPE

Have you expressed your aspiration to take on things at a higher level? Have you had conversations with those that are in a position to help you connect to the work or to the people at the next level to get you there? That's a lot of work on the individual. And many don't realize that in order to seize the career that they want, they have to have demonstrated an expressed ability, aspiration, and engagement. In the context of this book, *you're being your own career advocate*. It's that you need to have the ability, the aspiration, and the engagement. And it needs to be not only demonstrated but also expressed.

The future can seem distant, scary, overwhelming, or uncertain. It can also be exciting, hopeful, inspiring, and meaningful. You can take small steps now to set yourself up for happiness and success years down the road just by looking within. Open this next section to begin mapping out your ideal future.

IF YOU DON'T ASK FOR WHAT YOU WANT…

Don't be surprised by what you don't get. Don't be disappointed by not achieving results that you didn't put in the work to get.

"If you don't A-S-K, you don't G-E-T." Mind reading is just not something that you can expect from your manager. And that there are a lot of people that I've met in my career who expect that their leader or that the organization knows exactly what they want. How can I give you something that I don't know that you want? *More importantly, speak it to those who could potentially help you achieve it.* Or speak to those who have achieved what you want to achieve, who can tell you if you're going about it the right way or give you some suggestions for how you could do that.

a. What are three things you want in your career right now?

b. Think of a time when you wanted something but didn't ask for it - how did it make you feel? What would you do differently today?

c. When were you most disappointed in your career? How did you get past it?

d. Do you consider being an overachiever a strength or a weakness? Why?

DO YOU FEEL LIKE YOU'RE LEARNING SOMETHING?

If not, then it may be time to go.

I started asking myself. "You know what? Did I learn something new today?" I didn't have a 'yes' answer every day, but I gave myself this. After 30 days of asking myself if I learned anything new today, and the answer is no, it's time to go. I gave myself 30 days in a lot of places, and what did that turn into? That doesn't necessarily mean I just got up and left the organization. *But after 30 days, if I hadn't felt like I learned anything new, that might have fueled me to go to my leader and say, "Listen, I need something else to do."* Or "What are the projects I can work on?" "I think I've mastered this. What else do you have?"

a. If you could learn one thing at your current company right now, what would it be?

b. What critical knowledge, skill, or ability is currently missing from your repertoire?

c. When was the last time you did something for the first time at work?

d. If you could spend the next year mastering a particular skill, which one would you pick and why?

STARTING WITH 'IN MY EXPERIENCE' CAN'T BE CHALLENGED.

No one can tell you that you didn't have a life or career experience. But they can (and will) challenge your research, your thinking, and your feelings if you disagree with them.

In professional settings, people start to talk about their thoughts and feelings on matters. I've pushed back with, "You know what, that's interesting. I had a different experience." "Oh really?" By saying I have a different experience, people are now curious to see what your experience was. *They can't challenge what you have experienced because that experience is so very personal.*

a. When was a time that you were challenged on something at work?

b. Name a negative experience that you wish that you never had in your career.

c. What experience did you pass on that you wish you could go back to accept?

d. What experiences have shaped you the most in your career?

IT IS EASY TO WANT SOMETHING...

But being willing to do what it takes to get it is hard.

In finding the lack of willing, told me that, ultimately, I was chasing after something that I really didn't want. And the moment I got honest with myself, the stress of that fell away as well. *It's amazing how much stress can be caused by you not being honest with yourself.* Or not realizing who you are and not listening to yourself. I'm not willing to do this, which means I really don't want it. So I can either waste time fooling myself and others, or I can own it and let it go and move on.

a. Talk about a time when you started something but didn't finish it.

b. What have you wanted to do but took no action to achieve?

c. What have you failed at and had to admit that you didn't try your best?

d. What would you sacrifice to achieve your most lofty professional goal?

YOU SHOULDN'T WORK TO LIVE UP TO…

Someone else's definition of success. Find and pursue your own definition.

Most of the failures in my career came from trying to live up to someone else's definition of success for me. Trying to see myself and look my best in someone else's mirror instead of my own. Many times, I have lost before I even played the game. I think about success as just being at peace in the present for where you are. And you know what? *You don't need someone else's definition. You don't need someone else's validation. You need your validation.* Can you feel good about who you are and where you are, or can you not? Because to me, that's the ultimate definition of success. It's when you are at peace with yourself.

a. What is your definition of success in your professional life? In your personal life?

b. Does your day-to-day work connect with your definition of success?

c. Who is someone you know that lives their 'definition of success'?

d. What would need to change in your life for you to be living a life of success?

Now that you've made it this far in your candid interview with yourself, how are you feeling about what you've discovered about yourself? We know the prompts are making you think about things you've never thought about. Just sit for a moment and reflect on your findings before going into the last section.

FOSTERING YOUR KEY RELATIONSHIPS

As you go about all of the work that you do, you might do business with companies; but you are really doing business with people. As for growth, your boss could be someone that makes or breaks your next career opportunity. Being intentional about your relationships is imperative to your own success. You have to go through the stages of being known, being liked, being trusted, and then being referred or advocated for to build your relationship with those that can help you advance in your career. These points all impact your brand, your reputation, and how you are perceived throughout your career. The talisman of your career's success is based on the relationships you make along the way.

The time has arrived for you to cement together all of your self-learnings, reflections, and experiences with the all-important mortar of any successful career: the relationships you build along the way. The quality of these relationships is imperative to your growth and future. Prepare to dive into your past, present, and future to fully set yourself up for the career that you want to achieve.

LOOK FOR POWER BROKERS...

Notice with whom they associate. It is much more important who knows you, not who you know, that builds your professional brand.

What I suggest is going back to the first 90 days. Look, listen, and learn. Look for those who seem to be exemplars in the culture. The ones that people think highly of, the ones that are known for getting results, the ones that have a certain amount of influence, that they have a way about them, that they are basically iconic to the organization. And where it makes sense, try to find a way to interact with those people. What to say to somebody, "Listen, you know, I'm new to the organization, and I'm trying to understand how the organization does what it does. I'd love to have 15 minutes of your time. I'd love to ask you some questions and hear your answers and use that to help me navigate my way through this organization." So instead of you running around trying to say, "Oh, I know this person," we've all met those people who name drop. *Don't be the name-dropper. Be the one whose name gets dropped.* How do you go about doing that? You've got to get results. You've got to show up. You've got to be in the right place at the right time with the right message, the right attitude, and the right preparation. People will take notice.

a. What kind of personality do you work best with, and why?

b. How have you networked with someone above you at work before?

c. What's a time you disagreed with a decision that was made at work?

d. How do you manage stress in your daily work?

THE TRUE CHARACTER AND INTEGRITY OF...

A person will be revealed during moments of adversity.

When the stuff hits the fan, when the adversity hits, that's when you really find out what people are made of or what they're not. Adversity is something you can't plan for. All you can do is react to it. But what it means is this. *Those who have truly mastered emotional intelligence react to adversity the best.* Because they think back through the stages or the facets of emotional intelligence. In adversity, they try to get back to a place where they're very much self-aware. And at that moment, they self-manage. They realize that self-managing or managing themselves well has an impact on their social awareness and what people see of them, and how they see people. And that is focused on maintaining or fostering relationships.

a. How do you handle working with people who annoy you?

b. Tell me about a time when you had a conflict with a coworker.

c. Describe a time you got angry at work.

d. Describe a time when your work was criticized.

LEADERSHIP IS ABOUT...

Connecting with people.

Either it's a shared goal, a shared enemy, a shared accomplishment, what have you. How do you connect? At that moment, they connected, you know, the leaders that we had at that moment, connected with us because we were all in the navy. We all chose to join, and we all want to succeed. We all want to graduate from boot camp. And that connection was, "I will help you do all of those things. But to do all those things, you have to do this a certain way." That's how they had us. You connected because you connected with each person's intrinsic and extrinsic motivations. *All of us want to be led by people that we have a connection with, that we trust, and that we respect.* And if anytime someone is wondering if they are receiving that from you, you're not leading them.

a. How would your current boss describe you?

b. Describe a time when you had to give a person difficult feedback.

c. Tell me about a time you disagreed with a decision. What did you do?

d. What is the best way to get to know someone at work?

LEADERS LOOK FOR…

The best way to communicate with each of their people. Communication is not a one-size-fits-all task.

Most business issues are people issues. Why? Ultimately, because of communication. Communication should start with the person or the persons that are receiving the message. *How do I craft a message so that the people that I'm speaking with get what they need?* It's as much about what you're communicating as it is about how not thinking that you can send the grand email and it'll answer all of the questions that people may have. You have to target your communications for the audience. Realize that you always have more than one audience. Even if it doesn't appear to be so. There are more people looking and listening to what you say and what you don't say than you can imagine.

a. What adjectives would your past coworkers use to describe you and why?

b. How do you manage your time and stay organized?

c. Describe a time you went out of your way to help somebody.

d. Tell me about a time you demonstrated leadership skills.

LEADERSHIP AT THE HIGHEST LEVEL IS...

Thinking about the success of the business as a whole, in the order of the business first, of the team second, and of yourself last.

There's a theme here. Again, military here. The motto of the ship was "Ship. Shipmate. Self." And it was a reminder to always think about what's for the good of the ship first, what's for the good of my shipmate second, and then what's good for me third. *Not because you don't count, but it was the idea that if you're doing what's best for the ship, everybody wins. If you're doing what's best for your shipmate, everybody wins. And if you do those two things, you're already doing what's best for yourself.* Company. The team. And then myself. It was a great parallel, and it's carried with me through this day. It's the fact of looking at it as a funnel. Think about the wide-open end and working to the narrow end. Let's talk about the organization. Let's think about our team, and then finally, let's think about the individual later.

a. Describe a time you went above and beyond at work.

b. Tell me about the last time a coworker or customer got angry with you. What happened?

c. Do you think you could have done better in your last job?

d. Do you connect with the work that your business does? With your team?

Congratulate yourself on making it through *Things I Heard Myself Say: Insights from A Candid Interview with Yourself!* What you've asked of yourself is no easy feat - you should be proud of yourself and the personal courage it took to look directly into the mirror and answer questions that may have empowered you to meet your authentic self for the first time. With this greater self-understanding, we hope that you are one step closer to creating the career and life that you truly want!

CLOSING THOUGHT

Your journey to career success won't end with completing this journal! If you're interested in continuing your self-discovery, check out even more material on www.ThingsIHeardMyProfessorSay.com. You can also follow Eli Boulous and Dr. Curtis Odom on LinkedIn, Forbes, Fortune, etc. for more insight on owning your personal and professional development.

Quotes don't work unless you do ...

So, what are you going to do?

ABOUT THE AUTHORS

ELI BOULOUS

Eli Boulous is currently a Client Services Associate in the Manager Development Program at AlphaSights in New York City.

Hailing from a diverse and unique upbringing in Easton, PA, Eli has spent time growing and developing himself in Europe, the Middle East, and Asia while working in a variety of industries, including finance, technology, and real estate.

Formerly an employee of the UBS Investment Bank, marketing technology startup-turned-public Braze, and BDR of the Year at Gremlin Inc, Eli now commits his time to helping new members of the workforce discover their own definition of 'success' as they look to provide greater leadership for the communities they serve.

As the co-author of the books *Things I Heard My Professor Say* and *Things I Heard Myself Say*, Eli focuses on leveraging themes such as authenticity, empowerment, and personal development to uplift his peers and build the next generation of leaders!

DR. CURTIS ODOM

Dr. Curtis Odom is an Executive Professor of Management in the D'Amore-McKim School of Business at Northeastern University.

Educated as a scholar-practitioner, Dr. Odom's experiences as a management consultant inform both his research and teaching philosophy. Curtis believes that learning should be experiential and participant-centered and seeks to motivate, inspire, and instill in his students a sense of ownership of their learning journey. His ability to connect academic content to workplace and workforce context is born of a 20-year industry career as a corporate executive, entrepreneur, management consultant, and executive coach.

Away from Northeastern, Curtis is an international award-winning business transformation executive and acclaimed management consultant who provides pragmatic advice, coaching, and guidance to company executives, senior leaders, and management teams. He is often called to lead targeted business transformations by helping iconic organizations compete both more effectively and efficiently or make a strategic pivot. Curtis partners with his clients often during the bold, seismic shifts that an organization must make to both accelerate and execute change and strategic growth beyond typical measures or incremental advancements.

Prior to his industry and academic careers, Curtis served on active duty for 10 years in the United States Navy, which included being deployed during Operation Desert Storm.

CPSIA information can be obtained
at www.ICGtesting.com
Printed in the USA
LVHW100541100622
720955LV00005B/483

9 798986 085906